LIFE GOES ON

LIFE GOES ON

Poetry for Everyday People

Larry W. Winston

Copyright © 2008 by Larry W. Winston.

Library of Congress Control Number: 2008909800
ISBN: Hardcover   978-1-4363-8237-3
              Softcover   978-1-4363-8236-6

All rights reserved. No part of this book may be reproduced or transmitted in any form or by any means, electronic or mechanical, including photocopying, recording, or by any information storage and retrieval system, without permission in writing from the copyright owner.

This book was printed in the United States of America.

To order additional copies of this book, contact:
Xlibris Corporation
1-888-795-4274
www.Xlibris.com
Orders@Xlibris.com
55096

CONTENTS

LADIES

Sweet Sorrow 13
Don't Wait 14
Slow Down 15
Anywhere but Here 16
Suzy Bunny Tail 17
It's a Miracle 18
Mom (rules) 19
The Best Laid Plans 20
Rest Up 22
Once again, I'm sorry 23
Hush 24
Women 26
At Last 28
Smile 30
"You" 31
"The Lady of the House" 32
Jimmy 34
Sign language 36
Wrong turn Charlie 38

GENTLEMEN

Michaels` Big Mistake 43
A Fool and His Money 44
I Mean It! 46

Naive Steve...48
Regrets 50
Brothers from a Different Father 52
Ready to Take Off 54
The Time Bandit 55
To Cupid from Stupid..56
Captain in Training 58
I'll Stop This Car 59
The Pill 60
Give Me a Break...61
The Bank Officer Speaks 62
Leroy for president 64
I'm Not Well 66
Help!..68
Lets Not 69
Shoes..70
The Rose is off of the Vine:...72
$ Priceless $..74
Mans Best Friend 76
Hanky Panky..78
Pay Day...79

AND CHILDREN

The Interview...83
Life Goes On..84
The Answer..86
Two Kids at a Bus Stop..88
It's the Thought..90
Nice Try 92
Tex..94
A Penny for Your Thoughts 96
Mr. Irresponsible 98
Mom !...99

Mr. President..100
Queen of the Sideline...102
Dear Mom and Dad,..104
Simply the Best 106
The Pots Melting..107
Backward March 108
Fred...109
Lucky Me..110
6 Going on 60..112
Angels without Wings 114
That's Disgusting 115
The Gambler: 2nd grade can be tough 116

Dedication

There are too many people to individually thank for their support. I would however like to acknowledge the matriarch of my family, Mary Louise Winston, my inspiration and rock; my late father Edward Sr. (Thanks, Dad.) My late brother Mark, you're not forgotten; give Frank a hug from all of us. Thanks to my oldest brother, Edward Jr. Thanks for your steady wisdom; I've learned so much from you.

My brother Paul, you were the man even when we were boys. Celeste, my oldest sister, thank you for your encouragement. Thanks to Josephine, our second mother. Thanks to Donna, my unconditionally loving inspiration. Timmy, my younger twin, keep up the good work, continue to make us proud. Kimberly, my youngest sister, you made us all very proud. My son James, my source of pride, thank you. My daughters Roz, whose wise beyond her years, and Debbie, thanks for always being there. Diamond, little Jimmy, Jabreel, Christopher and all of my grandchildren, make us proud. I'm also dedicating this book to all of my cousins, nephews, nieces, aunts, uncles, friends, and extended family. I can't forget my little helpers Laurie and little Lauri; thank you so much. And Mary, my lifesaver at Dr. Sahovey's office.

I hope these poems make all of you smile because that's what I do when I think of you.

LADIES

Sweet Sorrow

With a warm gentle breeze on a somber cloudy day
The time has come when we must say good-bye
Let's be strong, keep our heads up
And let's both try not to cry
I warned you this day was coming
I told you it would be hard for us
I've been through this three times before
Separating like this is always very tough, but
We'll be back together soon
We'll get through this the best we know how
When I see your beautiful face again
My love will burst through my smile
Let's both stay calm, confident, and cool
As I proudly watch you walk through that door
Congratulations on your first day of school my child
Listen to your teacher and I'll see you back here at four

Don't Wait

Don't wait, when opportunity knocks, grab it with both of your hands
Don't wait, when a woman needs you, step up and be a man
Don't wait, when you see a child hungry, feed his belly and his soul
Don't wait, when you see a heart broken, do your best to make it whole
Don't wait, when you see a man down on his luck, give him a dime or two Because but for the grace of God, that man could be you
Don't wait, when you see someone lonely, go over and be a friend
To not comfort that lonely soul would surely be a sin
Don't wait, tell someone that you love them
You never know one day it may be too late
That's why I'm telling you I love you now
I'm so glad I didn't wait

Slow Down

Do you ever stop to enjoy the view
Do you have a passion for life and love too
When's the last time you've looked up to the sky
And admired a beautiful bird flying high
Do you enjoy the clean air after a rainy day
Have you kicked back in the park in the month of May
Do you rush through life without a care
Never stopping to marvel at it all
Have you forgotten your friends both far and near
Never stopping to give them a call
Maybe one day before it's too late
You should stop and take in the view
And appreciate God's great, green, beautiful earth
And be thankful it was created for you

Anywhere but Here

Somewhere there's children singing, somewhere birds chirp in the trees
Somewhere there's happy kids playing, others doing good little deeds
There's even quiet children reading and studying their history books
Somewhere there's girls in the mirror checking out their darling sweet looks
That's not the case in this house, that's not the case in this home
These kids don't want to go out and play, they'd rather stay in than roam
These monsters are driving me crazy, why did I agree to stay?
Never will I babysit this brood again, not even for twice the pay!

Suzy Bunny Tail

We called her Suzy Bunny Tail, she was always hopping around
Over here, over there, she never settled down
She may have come from Utah or somewhere up in Maine
She could have come from Panama, possibly from Spain
She was always in our business, never minding her own
She was up and down this street of ours, rarely was she at home
We used to talk about her and criticize her style
We'd roll our eyes when she would pass, she'd counter with a smile
We had no idea we'd miss her when she left our little town
We see how important she was to us, now that she is not around
She kept an eye on our children, house and property
When she was here there was no theft or no burglary
We`ve invested in safer mailboxes to secure our precious mail
We really miss that fine lady, Mrs. Suzy Bunny Tail

It's a Miracle

You may not have my eyes or nose, and it's easy to tell us apart
No, you may not have my eyes or nose, but you'll always have
    my heart
I'm not your biological father, and I wasn't there at your birth
But there's nothing that can lessen my love for you, nothing
    here on earth
No, you don't have my eyes or nose, and it's easy to tell us apart
But, my dear child, it's a medical fact, you'll always have my heart.

Mom (rules)

I didn't like the rules in our home; I questioned them all the time. Why couldn't Mom just leave me alone. I thought I was doing just fine. Pick up this, put down that, don't drink out of the carton, use a glass. Eat your breakfast, brush your teeth, hurry up or you'll be late for class. Why did she care if I was late for class? Use a glass for what? My lips were clean. Why was she always bossing me around? I thought it was because she was mean. Now that I'm older I've noticed a few things. I'm never late, I'm always on time. The last time I went to the dentist, she said my teeth were just fine. I treat others as I want to be treated. I hold doors open for those who want me to. Now I understand why mom's rules were so needed. They made me a better person . . . who knew?

The Best Laid Plans

I had it all planned, right down to a tee
There would be no ifs, ands or buts
I was just as confident as confident can be
My plan would get me out of my rut
I was going to get up and go for a jog
come back home and then
Eat a good breakfast, work out a bit
And be on the road by ten
I was going to go shopping, meet friends for lunch
My plan was perfect, you'd have been proud of me
I was going to buy plants and flowers for the yard

And a load of Catnip for (my cat) Fluffy
But jogging was out because it rained
No shopping, the rain ruined that too
Paying bills is out of the question
I found my dollars are down to a few
The cat ran away, no need for catnip
So I cancelled plans on going to the store
Please excuse me, I'm going back to sleep
Just roll me over, if I begin to snore

Rest Up

Don't just do something, sit there
Let me do all the work and chores
I wouldn't want any sweat, to come out of your precious pores
Let me continue to work day and night until the day I die
You just sit back and relax, have some milk and apple pie
Watch some TV, while I mow the lawn, kick your feet up and take a load off
Let me fluff your pillow up, we want it nice and soft
You say you'll look for a job tomorrow if the weather continues to be nice
You say the pie was pretty tasty and you'd like another slice
Well, here you go, eat, enjoy, your wish is my command
Don't get up, I'll bring you a towel to wipe your soft, smooth hands
Since you like to sit and read, I have something that may interest you
I made additional copies for your lazy sister and brother too
It's a copy of my will I'm not leaving you kids a dime
I'm leaving you kids the pleasure of work
Since you thought the pleasure was all mine

Once again, I'm sorry

You'd have your shape if it weren't for me.
I'm never right and you're never wrong
You want to trade me in for a purple Mercedes,
And your list of my faults are long
You want me to laugh when you laugh, cry when you cry
And dream all of your lofty dreams
Buy you fur coats, Platinum watches and sparkling diamond rings
Work while you sleep cuddle a while, and when the check
    comes pay with a smile
You're great at pointing out what's wrong with me
But my dear, this is what I I need
A little more appreciation would help
Cutting down on the nagging would be fine
If you can keep your insults to yourself
I`ll continue to do the same with mine

Hush

Hush, my child, please don't cry
I'm cold and very scared too
I'm taking you to a better life
a new start for me and you
If we're found you'll be taken from me
And I'll have no more reason to live
Don't move, stay still under these wet leaves
I'm so sorry, it's the only protection I can give
If I had a choice you wouldn't be here at all
No one deserves to be born into slavery

The master forced himself on me, behind his estate walls
I tried, but I couldn't fight him off, please forgive me
Hush, I hear the dogs and those men with their hanging ropes
I'm so afraid that we will be caught
For you. I have so many dreams and hopes
I couldn't bear ever seeing you bought
Yes, sleep my child, in a few hours it will be dawn
By then we should arrive at the safe home
One day I pray this country wakes up
And accepts us as one of their own

Women

Women—we guys will never figure you out. Why is it every time you ask us to do something, you always have to shout? Granted, you usually have to ask, to put it mildly more than once, but you don't have to talk to us guys like we're some kind of dunce. And we men don't understand, that whole toilet seat thing. Doesn't it take as much energy to put it down as it does to leave it up and viciously complain? And that whole thing, that women can do anything better than a man, don't brag. Most of the things that we can do, even a monkey can. Don't get me started on driving, you say you drive as well as us. All of the accidents that men get into—I wouldn't bring that subject up! And you say we never notice, when you get a new hair do or a dress. We don't even notice things on us, that's why most of the time we look a mess. Birthdays and anniversaries, you want us to remember that too. Sometimes we don`t remember to check our socks; we've been known to wear a brown and a blue.

Crying at weddings and movies, we'll never figure that out. We'd rather be at a boxing match watching a poor guy get knocked out! We men work really hard, to buy our boys things like tuxedos, for their proms, but every time they score touchdowns, they always yell "Hi Mom" And Valentine's day is for women, but we understand, we know we owe you gals the world. That's why we don't mind. if we just get a card, even though we gave you pearls. We do know, if it weren't for women, this world would not run as smooth as it does now. Cooking and cleaning and so much more, and you do it with a smile. It's amazing, a thank you is all you want to be paid, even though you're the family's doctor, psychiatrist, and selfless maid. If we men were held to your standards, you'd always see us pout. But a simple "THANK YOU" is all you women request, nope . . . we'll never figure you out!

At Last

Excuse me, is this the place where I go to vote?
I thought it was but I wasn't sure.
I'm 96, this is the first time I'll vote.
I feel Barack will help all of us poor.
I've been through a lot in my 96 years,
There was a time I couldn't vote because of my skin, When I
    think of that time, my eyes fill with tears.
We knew our place, we were second class citizens.
Martin Luther King helped paved the way, Like others who
    fought for us his blood was spilled, I never dreamed this
    day would come, You see, anyone who helped us was killed.

I couldn't sleep last night, I was too excited!
But I'm energized, I feel Like a kid!
We're making history, I'm so delighted, No longer do I have to keep my feelings hid.
The line is getting shorter, I'm getting nervous again.
We're closing the door on our ugly past, I'm so proud of How far our country has made it.
I'm shaking, this day`s here at last.
Do I look alright? Let me take off my coat, If Obama wins I know will cry.
Well, I'm up next, I'm going into vote
I made it, I'm so proud, good-bye.

Smile

When she was three, she scraped her knee,
I laughed and laughed till I cried
I guess that was only normal, you see, I was only five
We went to school together, I was always two grades ahead
I showed no interest in her, but she was always in my head
I graduated high school, and off to college I went
She stayed home and went to college, and worked to pay her rent
On holidays Id return from school, I'd visit her for a while
I never showed how much I cared, though, she made my
    young heart smile
I'm pretty sure I loved her, I think she loved me too, but
I was young and kind of dumb, I played down my affections as
    young men often do
She got tired and finally moved on, and with her my hopes and dreams
Playing the strong, silent type was a very stupid scheme
I must admit moving on was a very smart thing she did
It made me realize, that it's not wise, to keep your feelings hid
She taught me a sobering lesson, She made me pursue her for
    quite a while
But now that she's let me catch her again, our hearts share the
    same big smile.

"You"

You carried me when I couldn't walk
You were the tonic that made me strong
You spoke for me when I couln't talk
You reassured me when my confidence was gone You encouraged me with everything you said You were always there never leaving my side You chased ghosts from underneath my bed You held me close when I needed to cry You always provided me a home You made me the person I am today, With You I've never felt alone You are perfect in every way. You're my angel on earth, and my best friend. Whenever you need me just count to three. Not just today, but until the very end, You can always count on me.

"The Lady of the House"

He said he'd satisfy her need for speed, With a bus pass, to get her to the store.
And if she was a good little wife,
There was a small chance that she could earn more.
He insisted that she do more housework,
And be a better mother to his six kids.
And even though none of those kids were hers, It was important that they all be well fed.
He says if he strays once in a while, grow up!
After all, he's just a man.

Then he asked her "By the way, did you bring in the garbage cans?"
He said he's tired of explaining that the girl he was kissing, was
    an old family friend.
He said, "Why don't you go do the laundry?"
And to please stop bugging him,
But she's finally figured out a way, to get everything that she seeks.
And "Mr. Big Stuff" and his kids won't be laughing much
    longer, Because she's divorcing them all next week!

Jimmy

You can`t tell me the meaning of life
I can`t even leave you alone at night
You`re very demanding every day
Do you appreciate me? you don`t say
Did you thank me for the meal I prepared for you?
No, all you did was burp, when you were through Well baby, let
me tell you something . . . and I mean this from my heart

Now just listen to me, before your crying starts, I'll tell you the meaning of life . . . the meaning of life, is you. And there's no sadness, anger or regrets, when our long day is through. And when you burp over my shoulder, I sigh, and I can't ever leave you, with out my wanting to cry. Who would have thought someone so tiny, would generate the love of three. Who would have thought some one so precious, would ever be a part of me. You're my own little baby, and you're two months old. When you're in my arms, my world's not cold. Now lie down to sleep, my little one, and God . . . Thanks again, for my beautiful son

Sign language

I've got a question, I hope that you don't mind, I'm pretty sure you've heard this before "Hey goodlook'n what's your sign, I'll tell you mine if you tell me yours".
Some people are awfully proud of their signs, Others say I don't believe in that stuff, Some can take it or leave it While others just can't get enough There's earth, water, air and fire, the four elements of the zodiac Earth and water are emotional and fair, air and fire intellectual and laid back I've noticed that everyone agrees, when their readings say they're just fine And quickly, become non believers, when it says their personality is out of line But really, we are all emotional beings, we express ourselves in different ways Some freak out when they get upset, others seem hardly fazed

The waters are controlled by the moon, and the moon controls the sea and tides Since our bodies are mostly water the moon takes us all for a ride When there`s a full moon the werewolves come out, the hospitals and jails become full Just ask the doctors and policemen, they say that it`s natures rule As far as compatibility goes, some signs go better with others I have some advice for you all, my cosmic sisters and my cosmic brothers The next time you`re asked "what`s your sign"? answer and take a chance, It could be the start of a heavenly friendship, or an out of this world romance.

Wrong turn Charlie

Today our divorce is final, I didn't think I'd feel this way, I thought I'd be feeling much more joy. I was planning to celebrate. But I'm having this funny feeling, I'm feeling some sadness too. After all of those court room dealings, I feel sick as if I have the flu You got the house the kids and the pool. And I get to pay your bills. I'm moving to a basement apartment. You're` remaining in Beverly Hills

They'll call me a dead beat dad and you the long suffering wife. I'm beginning to feel suicidal, I'm afraid to go near the knives You'll be interviewing potential husbands. I won't be able to afford a cheap date The judge has threatened to jail me. If my alimony payment is late. I think I've come to my senses. I'm asking you for another chance. If you promise to work on your temper. I'll work on that thing, called romance

GENTLEMEN

Michaels' Big Mistake

Son . . . you can kill moose, meese, ducks and geese You can even snare a bear.
You can kill chickens, hogs, coons, and frogs Squirrels and even deer.
But son, you done went and harmed a dog
You coulda killed somethin' on our long list And that woulda been just fine.
But you done gone and killed mans best friend And dang it that's where we draw the line.

A Fool and His Money

I'm my grandpa's nephew's sister's boy
It's a little hard to explain
Yeah, I'm Bubba and Bertha's bundle of joy
I was a problem, at least that's what they claim
I admit a little more manners I could use
A thank you here or there wouldn't hurt
When anything's missing, I'm accused
My dear family treats me like dirt
At least that was up until a week ago
When the dear family got the news
Now my sister brings me cookies and tea
And my aggressive brother shines my shoes

Lately, Bertha and Bubba are loving
I didn't think it was in them . . . who knew?
But I have news for them all
I'm leaving this house tonight
I'm getting on the first thing smoking
I'm taking an early flight
I hit the lottery big, I'm not giving them a dime
I'm sneaking out tonight, I'll have a real good time
But first, Celeste and I, are going to go shopping
To purchase a new car and fur
She said she'll help me with my money
And don't trust anyone else, but her.

I Mean It!

Take this money and don't give it back. I don't care how much I beg or plead
Even if I curse or yell at you, keep that cash far away from me
We were in the casino for less than an hour, we won, it's time to go home
Don't give me a dime of that money no matter how much I beg or moan
There's a lot of things we can do with this cash. Pay bills or take a trip to Italy. I'm telling you, no matter what I say, keep that loot far away from me.

You know, honey, it's still early, and I feel like I`m
> still lucky.
I was just thinking, I may have miss spoke when
> I said hide that money from me. I feel lucky
> tonight, you need to give me back that stash.
I know what I said before, dear, now I'm telling you,
> hand over the cash.
I'm well aware of what I said previously, but I'm
> telling you this right now. Let me have what's
> rightfully mine, or I will get embarrassingly loud.
> Thank you, darling, I'll be right back. I'll double
> this money, you'll see.
And darling when I hand you the winnings, please
> take it quickly, and don't give it back to me!

Naive Steve

I borrowed some money from a guy I met, he
    lent it in a blink of an eye
When he asked for repayment, I started to sweat
'Cause I soon learned he's not a very nice guy
I said I know I owe you $500
And in a few days, I'll gladly pay you back
The guy said, "It was $500 a week ago,
Now you owe me much more than that."
He said, "There's interest I forgot to add,
It's a hundred dollars, and that's no joke."
I laughed in his face, and he really got mad
He said pay up, then he gave me a poke
I called my dad to see what he had, he said don't
    call him anymore

So I told the guy, I can't pay. That's why i
 borrowed 'cause I'm really poor.
It's too upsetting to repeat what he said, but
 when he was through with his talk,
I asked, could he think of something else to do
 to me 'cause I'm going to need my knees to
 walk.
Well, I was so scared I robbed a bank, to pay
 that mean guy back
Now, I'm serving ten years in jail, wondering
 how I got so offtrack
So, my friend, if you ever ask someone for
 money, consider how badly it could end.
Take it from me, never borrow money, it's much
 safer and wiser to lend.

Regrets

Wow, my first day in heaven, what a beautiful sight. I'm entering these pearly gates, I'm praying with all of my might. I'm wondering what my wife's going through? My kids must really be sad. Why was I so selfish? I could have been a better dad. I could have cherished my wife more and treasured her everyday

I could have been more attentive, there's so many things I didn't say.

If I could just go back there, I'd be a better husband to my wife

I'd make sure my kids were happier and had a better life

I wouldn't act as if my life was just a little game

All of the people I ignored, I'd learn each of their precious names

I'd appreciate the birds, the trees, the flowers, and I'd learn to love myself

I'd put my petty ego way up high on a distant shelf
I miss my family so much, I can hear my wife
    calling me
I can hear her lovely voice.
Oh my, could it be?
Yes! I was merely dreaming, I'm really still here in bed
It was all a dreadful nightmare, thank goodness
    I'm far from dead
Tomorrow, I'll tell everyone I know, how glad I
    am that they're in my life.
My kids, my friends, my neighbors, and my very
    precious wife
I'll earn my way to heaven now that I'm so very
    much alive
I'll leave no doubt that I belong in heaven, the
    next time that I arrive.

Brothers from a Different Father

Welcome to my world, wipe your feet, and come on in
Did you have a hard time finding the place?
Though you don't know me, one day we could be friends
My world can be filled with fear and doubt and unrealistic dreams
And people who have no idea, what loving their fellow man means
We have people here who have given up, feeling life has let them down.
Welcome to the ghetto, come on in, and look around
Do you think we're here because we're lazy and have no pride
It's true we're both from this town, just born on different sides
I didn't invite you over to my world to bring your spirits down

I just want to discuss what seems to be holding us good folks down
I'd like your opinion on an issue, I hope you don't feel uncomfortable and leave
I want to know if you think you're better than us, is that what you truly believe?
And if you are better than us, shouldn't you be helping us out
Instead of putting the less fortunate down and flexing all of your clout
Maybe you should leave before it gets dark, my world can be a frightening place
Though the neighborhood is showing improvement it's at a very gradual pace
When you go back home, will you tell all of your friends that you see?
That they're all invited over, I think they should get to know me
Bye now, thanks for coming, I hope someday our worlds will meet
And my friend, think about this: but for the grace of God, my shoes could have been on your feet.

Ready to Take Off

I'd love to fly in a luxurious plane
The sky would be my friend
A trip to France, Italy, and Spain
I could fly to Egypt and Finland
I'd fly to Barbados, a few days in Greece
I'd enjoy my journey in both comfort and in peace
No more anxiety, only bliss
The sky would be my highway to happiness
At the drop of a hat, I'd take off day or night
Never stopping to consider the time
I'd hop on plane no mater what flight
For absolutely no reason or rhyme
But I won't be seeing France, Greece, or Spain
No, it's sad to say I won't be flying anywhere
Just the thought of me boarding any airplane
Makes my adventurous heart fill with fear.

The Time Bandit

I thought you were my friend, I thought we were okay
We did everything together, we partied everyday
I'll do anything you ask, but I can't stop breaking the law
I beg of you don't tell the cops, please don't make me crawl
I don't want to break the law, I don't want to do these crimes
But it sure beats working for a living, and it saves a lot of time.

To Cupid from Stupid

According to my teachers, I'm not stupid. According to my mom, I'm a handsome guy. But I'm leaving my love life up to cupid. 'Cause I can't get a date though I've tried. I get shy and tense when I see a girl I would marry. My face gets red as if I've been crying. I can't get out the words *hi, my name is Larry*. So you can see why whatever I'm selling, they're not buying. So cupid help me snag a lady—a charming, old-fashioned kind of gal. I don't want a woman who's shady. I'd like a woman with a very sweet smell. I'm too lazy to work though we'll need money. I'll do the housework and bring in the mail. And, cupid, it's a plus if she's funny. And make sure she has a job that pays well.

While you're at it, I'd like if she didn't talk much. You see, I'm going to need my quiet time. I don't want a drunk, don't send me a lush. A prim-and-proper tea totler will be fine. While your at it, make sure she's nice and slim with the works, if you know what I mean. I'm going to insist that she's tidy, organized, neat, and clean. If she has any kids, don't bother, I need all of the attention for myself. It's okay if she has sisters, no brothers, once again a plus if her family has wealth. Cupid, I know I'm asking a woman for a lot, but I think I deserve the best. I'd go out and help you look, but I'd rather stay home and rest.

Captain in Training

I enrolled in a class to become a superhero, I wanted to rescue fair maidens in distress. I practiced every move the instructor gave me.
I worked hard, there was no time for rest. I lifted weights and exercised to get stronger. I suffered weeks learning how to fall.
I don't want to be a superhero any longer. In the morning, I'll give Capt. Suplex a call.
The outfit he sold me looks like pajamas, and the mask is two sizes too small.
I tried the captain's moves out on the guy next door. He blackened both of my eyes in the short fight.
I'm sad to say it's been a week, and I'm still sore, but I think I'm regaining my sight.
I'm going to ask the captain for a refund. Being a superhero is not for me. I hope he doesn't get mad and harm me when I ask him to refund my enrollment fee.
A new school just opened up, down the block, they`re teaching how to plant and grow trees.
I'll enroll as soon as I'm able to walk because the neighbor broke both of my knees.

I'll Stop This Car

Don't make me stop this car and come back there. We're trying to enjoy this ride. Jimmy, get back over there, and Diamond, stay on your side. Look at all of the scenery. Every time you scream, there's something else you miss. Now say your sorry for yelling in his ear and give your brother a kiss. There will be no swearing in this car, you had better watch what you say. Just relax and enjoy the ride, it's such a lovely day. Who wants ice cream? Well then, you had better settle down. Diamond, you have such a pretty face, why the big sad frown? Jimmy, why are you crying? Let's have fun you guys. Diamond, sit up straight. Jimmy, dry your eyes. I can't understand you. What are you guys trying to say? You say we have to turn back. Turn around, we're going the wrong way? Oh no! I just realized why you're so upset. I was so busy with you and your brother, we have to go back, I completely forgot, and drove off without your mother.

The Pill

The label on the bottle said, "SERIOUS SIDE EFFECTS BEWARE." Knowing what the risk were, I still took those pills without fear. Turns out the pills I took were dangerous—yes, very dangerous indeed. They made me very weak. I now crawl on both hands and knees. I have gotten sneers and chuckles, from both neighbors and so-called friends. Not one of them have attempted to be kind. The control I once had over my bowels, thanks to those pills, are no longer mine. I've been hospitalized for a month now. I witnessed the doctors and nurses laugh when they think I don't see. I shake for no apparent reason, and have two unreliable kidneys. But even though those pills have weakened my kidneys and given me suicidal thoughts, I honestly just don't care. Because I'll have the last laugh if those pills really work and grows me a full head of hair.

Give Me a Break

The only luck I have these days are always bad
I'm so unlucky I misplaced the only friend I've ever had
I play the lottery everyday, the same numbers 2-5-8
Then one day i didn't play, of course it came out straight
A man stopped me in the middle of the street and said, "Smile, things could be worse"
While smiling I got hit by a car
Things really did get worse
Now I'm in an ambulance that by the way just hit a tree
I don't know how much more of this bad luck I can take
I'm wondering when something good will finally happen to me
Until then this is the decision I ultimately will have to make
I'll need to be more specific, I'll be more careful in what I say
    Because when I wished for a break last night, I didn't mean my leg

The Bank Officer Speaks

Sir, how dare you accuse me
You're fired from this bank, go away
We have no more interest in anything you have to say
If we knew you were going to accuse me
We'd have asked you to leave before
Everyone, out of my way, I'm booting him out the door
Where's his coat get his hat, it's time to say
    good-bye
We had no idea you'd come to this meeting and
    fill our ears with lies
Cover his mouth, shut him up, bind, and gag
    him if you must
My dear coworkers, there's not a word he's uttered
    any of us can trust
Since no one's going to assist me in kicking him out
At least please listen to me. Okay, it's true I was
    in the vault
Where all of the money was, and yes, I was able
    to purchase
A fur hat with matching gloves. And sure, I
    bought a car

That's big and beautiful and fit for a king, but,
    my dear friends, I can assure you.
It may look expensive, but this is a very cheap
    diamond ring
He's wrong I didn't buy this car outright, I
    purchased it on lease.
So what do you say dear friends, let's not involve
    the overworked police
Put that phone down, Bill, can't we work
    something out?
Do you want some season tickets? What's all
    this anger about?
I see you guys don't believe me, and you're right,
    I did borrow the cash
But I was going to pay it all back, every cent,
    right down to the last.
I'll turn my own self in. I knew I'd get caught
    after a while
I'll drive myself down to the police station, at least
    I'll arrive in style

Leroy for president

Leroy is our quarterback, he's going to save the day!
We're 10 yards from pay dirt, Leroy will lead the way
We love Leroy dearly, he won't let us down
We were up by 7 points earlier, we're down by 4
    points now
35 seconds left in the game, 4 downs to get it done
We're all much too nervous to be having any fun
Leroy's under center, Bubba Jones hikes the ball
Leroy hands it to our running back, who gets 3
    tough yards then falls
Second down and 7 Leroy takes 3 steps back,
    and heaves a perfect pass
In and out of our receivers hands, the crowd takes
    that bum to task
Third down, Leroy keeps the ball himself, and
    gets tackled at the 1 inch line
Leroy jumped up smiling, that's a very good sign.

Our beloved quarterback takes the ball from the center, 5 seconds left on the clock
Leroy hands the ball to our running back, closes his eyes and throws a crushing block
We don't like Leroy anymore, when he closed his eyes he hit the wrong man
He viciously hit our running back, knocking the ball right out of his hands
With one second left on the clock, the ball was handed over on downs
It was time to leave the stadium, some wiping tears others were sporting frowns
You know . . . it's funny about our heros', they're treated like gods by all of us fans
We once worshiped, Leroy, but he proved he's just a man.

I'm Not Well

Honey, don't panic! but I saw the doctor today. Sit down, take a deep breath, guess what he had to say! He said my blood pressure's up, and my stress level's killing me. He checked me from head to toe, then of course, he had to weigh me. I sat on the exam table for an hour, until the doctor came back with my results. He said my blood pressure's way too high. He asked, "When your wife cooks, does she use a lot of salt?" I was offended. I said, "My wife's a great cook, although everything she cooks is soaked in grease." He suggested that I eat out more, or my precious life is soon going to cease. He said to get my stress level down, I should go out more with the guys.

Guess what else he told me, dear, and boy was I surprised. He said I should play more golf and watch more sports on TV. And get a fast new sports car, that should bring down my stress gradually. He said when I'm slow to do what you ask, you should be more understanding. He said you should rub my feet, neck, and back, and you should try to be less demanding. So, honey, please run me a bath, set out my clothes, and don't wait up for me. I'm going to call some of the guys. The doctor said going to the "Gentlemens Club" would be a good form of therapy. Honey, you seem disturbed. Why are you looking at me like that. Now, dear, calm down, relax, put down that baseball bat. Sugarplum, I was just playing around, about what the good doctor had to say. You sit down, I'll rub your feet. I can see you've had a long day.

Help!

I'm riding with my neighbor, scared out of my mind
I'm more concerned about arriving alive
Than I am about being on time
Where'd he get his license from? Who okayed his drivers permit?
He's not qualified to be behind that wheel
He's a danger from where I sit
I'm going to wind up in a body cast
Whew! We almost hit that wall
I'ts my fault, he's driving this fast
I shouldn't have said any thing at all
I should have never mentioned to my neighbor, the cop
That there's a donut sale out at the mall

Lets Not

Lets do something about famine in the world
We could demand countries stop their quarrels
Or lets not, and say that we did
We could be fair when we report the news
We could respect each others points of views
Or lets not. and say that we did
Let talk about race in an open way
Lets make our justice system fair today
Or lets not, and say that we did
We could work together and stop silly fights
We could make our streets safer at night
Or not, and say that we did
Or we can continue to ignore others rights
We could turn a deaf ear to our fellow mans plight
We could do nothing and hope things get better on their own
And not get together and remain alone
But lets not, and say that we did

Shoes

Don't worry I wont bother you, that's what I could have said.
I could have given up on you, and just turned my head.
But I stuck with you through your rebellious years, And now your a respectable man.
Now it's your turn my son, to do all that a father can.
I'm asking you not to give up on your son, when he says your not welcome in his life.
Stick with him, make him strong, do a favor to his future wife.
It's tough raising kids it's not always easy, no one said that it would be fun.
But put into him, what I put into you, it's worth it my weary son.

I must admit, I enjoy watching you get, everything that you gave to me, Watching you read him "Hey Diddle Diddle" and being thanked with a lap full of pee.

And as he gets older watching you try to maintain, some of your common sense, When it appears the older he gets the more he makes you tense.

So good luck son, if you need me, don't call . . . Your Mother and I are going out to eat.

By the way, I've noticed you don't seem so sure of yourself now that my shoes are your fatherly feet.

The Rose is off of the Vine:

Hey Violet, hide the liquor Aunt Rose is coming tonight. One Aunt Rose and a fifth of anything equals an ugly fight. Hide the silverware we'll use plastic. We all know that Aunt Rose steals. We'll eat quickly and get her out of here this will be one fast Christmas meal. If she brings that guy she calls "Daddy" lets play like we're not at home cause' the last time she brought him with her, he stole mommy's phone. Shh . . ., peep out the window, is that Aunt Rose?

And see if she`s already drunk! She is? And he's staggering behind her? I knew it! Our Christmas is sunk! I'm going upstairs, I`m not staying down here. I refuse to participate in any more Christmas fights. So please, tell Aunt Rose I wished her a Merry Christmas, and to all of you a good night.

$ Priceless $

Though, that rich man doesn`t have a penny to his name. For him, a solitary penny is too much. It would be more money than he would ever need. To spend on houses cars, or clothing and such. There`s no need for him to take out any loan. He has no need to shop at the local mall. There`s no need to re-finance his modest home. He has no need for needing anything at all. There`s nothing more he needs to do here on earth.

He died this morning an extremely wealthy man. Money was not the measurement of his worth. He struck it rich with a very simple plan. He didn't worship money like a lot of people do. He gave to charities, and to any one in need. He was wise, he always used to say, "You can't take it with you" Leave your wallet, everything in heaven will be free

Mans Best Friend

There'll be no reason for sunshine tomorrow, A steady rain can come early and stay late.
I'm so sad, and my hearts filled with sorrow, I'm no longer concerned about my lifes fate.
The birds in the trees can stop singing, The proud eagle no longer need fly.
The church and school bells can stop ringing, It's not important if I live or die.
The milkman can stop his deliveries,
The mailman doesn't have to come today.

My once happy life is filled with misery, My happiness is on permanent delay.
This is the most sadness I've felt in years, I had no idea a loss could hurt so deep.
I no longer try to hold back my tears,
My tears flow, even when I'm fast asleep.
I'm so sorry, our loving marriage must end.
My heart is empty, there's a deep aching hole.
You've made it impossible to remain lovers and friends, Ever since you lost the remote control.

Hanky Panky

Hank, when I suspected my wife was cheating
You talked me out of it, your wisdom knows no bounds
If it weren't for you, I'd be more suspicious
My wife says, we're lucky to have you around
When I caught her coming out of that motel
You were right there standing by her car
And Hank, it's amazing, you were already there
When I caught her dancing on top of that bar
And when you suggested I go across town when I was looking for her
While you stayed in town to look
You found her and took her in for the night
My gosh Hank, you're a true friend in my book
You know it warms my heart Hank, to know that you're always
    somewhere close by
But it's strange, I always find you where my wife has just been
I can't figure that out, no matter how hard I try
Hold on Hank, I just put two and two together
Yes, Im finally starting to see the light
My wife always blushes and say's you're so amazing
And dog gonnit Hank, she's a liar, but this time my friend, she's right

Pay Day

Some jobs pay minimum wage,
Others pay a handsome sum.
Some jobs pay everyday,
Others only once a month.
A lot of people have jobs they truly hate,
They can't wait for the day to be through.
But they show up to work everyday,
Because they know that there bills will be due.
When you thanked me for doing a good job At raising you to become a man, I want you to know that it wasn't a job my son, But a joy, that I'd gladly do all over again.

AND CHILDREN

The Interview

I was asked to bring a beer to the man in charge
I thought I'd turn this meeting into an interview
I needed some income really, really bad
Along with the beer I brought my sixth-grade diploma too
The man in charge looked at me, and this is what he said.
Son, I told you to bring me a beer from the fridge, this is not
    an interview
There's no pay for working here. And don't walk on the back of
    your shoes.
Now go up stairs and take your bath, this time wash behind
    your ears.
When you're sixteen years old, you can get a real job
Now hand over that nice cold beer.

Life Goes On

I want to go to heaven
But I don't want to die
'Cause I'm only seven, if I go my Mom will cry
When my Dad went to heaven, my Mom cried everyday
When I asked her how far it was, she said it's far away
My Dad visits me in my dreams, and tells me he loves me so
He's always happy and playful, and says things I need to know
When I told my Mom about my dreams, I saw tears, and then she smiled
Mom's getting much better now, she hasn't cried for quite a while. Mom says we'll be with Dad again, when God calls us all back home

I'm sure glad Mom didn't go with him, and leave me all alone
Mom says the next time we`ll see Dad, is a long long time away
She says when ever I want to talk to him, just close my eyes and pray
And God will hear my prayer, and tell my Dad what I said
I usually talk to God at night, after being tucked in bed
It`s been nice talking to you, now I think I`ll go have some fun
I`ll be hunting my sister down, with my brand new water gun

The Answer

I sent two letters to Santa and God
I made sure I covered all of my bases
I didn't want a shiny new bike or those shoes
    with the fancy laces
I asked for something much bigger than that
I prayed they would answer my plea
I asked for something more precious than gold,
    and I wanted it immediately
Santa wrote back:
His elves couldn't make my wish come true, not
    even in a million days
He said, "I suggest you go to church my son, and
    get down on your knees, and pray."
So I went to church and prayed real hard
I said, "Dear God, my Grandpa's awfully sick.
    Please don't take him away from us, and get
    him home real quick."

Well, I'm very sad to say, when I got back home, I learned, Grandpa had passed away.

For a long time, I was mad at that old Santa, and I was pretty mad at God too

Till one day, Mom said, "Bobby, Santa sent you a letter, sit down, and I'll read it to you."

It said: "Dear Bobby, hello, this is Santa again. Thank you for writing me. God delivers the blessings and they don't fit under a tree.

"Now God blessed you for years, with Grandpa, and you enjoyed him everyday. Son, your Grandpa was ninety-six years old, how long did you expect him to stay? God rewarded him by taking him home.

"Once again, he's healthy and happy, my boy, knowing he's with our dear Lord now, son, should fill your heart with joy."

So, Bobby, the next time you kneel to pray, don't pray for blessings wrapped in bows.

Like your parents, God knows what's best for us all, so sometimes he just has to say no.

Two Kids at a Bus Stop

Hi, you don't know me, I'm from across the way
I come from a family who struggles, but we work hard everyday
Times aren't always bad, we have some good times too
Things could be much worse, I guess you say the same thing too
In my community, there's a lot of despair and pain
But it's getting much better now, there's been some important gains
It's not very often that I get anything new
But my family loves me, I`m sure yours loves you too
I have black skin, and you have white, but underneath we're
    both the same

When one of us hurts the other one, we both experience pain
Sadly, society sees us differently, though it's better than it was before
We've come a very long way, but we have to do so much more
No, we don't know each other, but I really think we should
I think we can be good friends, I really think we could
Let's make a serious effort, regardless of what others may say
Let's you and me be friends, and let's start that friendship today
You don't know me, and I don't know you
Heres my hand, for you to shake
Hi, my name is Larry, let`s make a bond that will never break

It's the Thought

We didn't have much money for your gift, Dad
Still, we hope this gift shows you how we feel
My quarter and Jo's dime is all we had
Oh yeah, Mommy pitched in a brand new dollar bill
She said she wanted to help us out, and that was fine
Though we wanted this gift to be, from just us two
It had to be an extra special present this time
We wondered, what would be the perfect thing for you
So we put our two heads together
And even though the problem seemed pretty tall

We thought, since we see you go to work in any weather
You deserved the very best gift of all
So we gave Mommy her dollar back
And bought you candy, with the money we had
I think we know why your smiling like that
'Cause you love us, and you're proud to be our Dad
You say this is the best gift you ever got?
And you'll take some candy, and give us the rest?
Okay, if you insist, we did buy a lot
We love you, Dad, happy father's day, you're the best!

Nice Try

Sir, Mom says you're my father, but I'm not quite so sure
Further investigation into this matter is required
Granted, I look exactly like you, dear sir.
But you could merely be an actor Mommy's hired
I'll have to insist on fingerprints, and we'll need some DNA
I'm sorry if my demands sound a little tough
Oh, I know that you and I carry around the same last name
But, my good man, that's not nearly good enough
I don't know, you could be fibbing about being my dear old dad
That's if Dad is even your real name
For all I know, you could be an imposter in our home
Let me do some research I'll see if our bloodline's are the same

I know we go through this every night just around bedtime
But you can`t blame me for trying, Mr. Smith
I'm eight-and-a-half years old, I should be able to stay up past nine
Do you have any idea how many TV shows you've made me miss?
Come on, Dad, can't we work something out? I need some
    more TV time
Your offer is if I don't go to bed, there'll be no allowance, not
    even one thin dime?
I guess I'll have to accept your proposal, and although it fills
    my heart with sorrow,
Good night, Mommy and Daddy, I love you both. I'll see you
    at breakfast bright and early tomorrow.

Tex

I'm a lawman, I keep those outlaws on the run. I carry six silver bullets, in my pearl-handled guns. I pay no attention to those bad guys petty little gripes. I'm tough and tall and mean. I'm your typical, strong, silent type. When those outlaws come to town, they learn quickly that I don't play. The saloon owners love me so much, I never have to pay. Now hold on to your hat pardners . . . now what? That`s my Mom's calling for me! I cant have any fun. Her name is Mommy. My name isJimmy, I'm her six-and-a-half-year-old son.

I better mount up and ride my horse, that she calls her kitchen
 broom. Where's my trusty stallion? Just as I thought, she
 stole him out of my room. I asked her as nice as I could,
 not to use him anymore.
I'm tired of her using my transportation, to sweep her dirty floors.
I'll just have to ride the mop, but I'll ride it with a frown.
 Uh-oh!
I gotta go, I hear my Dad calling me.
The real lawman in my town.

A Penny for Your Thoughts

I asked my mom, "Why is life filled with pain? And why it isn't always sunny, even when it rains? Why are some people rich and others poor? Why do countries fight? Why do we have war? Why do some live in mansions and others in boxes? That just doesn't seem fair! And, Mom, why is some people's hair curly, and others have very straight hair? Why are some people full of life, while others just want to die? And why can't we always be happy?

Why do some things in life make us cry? And why are our four little fingers different than our one lonely thumb? Here's a question for you, Mom, where do all of those darling babies come from?" Mom said, "I'm a little busy honey. Go ask your dad, see what he has to say." Dad reached for his wallet, gave me a five, and said, "Son, go outside and play." Well, so far I've racked up one hundred dollars. I'll ask a bunch of real embarrassing questions tonight. Now it's just a matter of time, before I have enough money, for a new bike.

Mr. Irresponsible

I'm not really sure where my homework has went
As for being late, I guess I just lost track of time
Even though my homework may have been taken by accident
I can't help but feel some responsibility, may be mine
I looked everywhere for that homework, I looked low and high
The reason I`m late every morning
Is its hard to tell my loved ones good-bye
If only I had more time I could elaborate
But I really must get going to my next class
You'd never forgive yourself if you made me late
Mrs. Brown, I know you want me to do well and pass
So I have an idea, this will make you feel good about yourself today
Don't call my mom, forget I was late, and please feel free to
    give me . . . an *A*

Mom !

Mom, it's finally snowing, I can't wait to go outside and play.
  I've waited six long months for this very snowy day.
Mom, could you help me with my snow suit, my boots, my
  hat, and gloves?
I can't wait to get out there, in that snow that I really love. Zip
  me up real good, Mom, and guide me to the door.
Wow, I've got so many clothes on, I feel nice and warm.
But first could you yell outside and tell my friends I'll be out soon?
And then can you quickly help me out of these clothes? I think
  I need to use the bathroom.

Mr. President

Dear Mr. President,

I'm writing you for help today 'cause times are kinda tough. We're on a food and money diet. Mom says stay strong though times are rough. I put on a brave face when I'm in school 'cause the kids would be mean if they knew. Mom says kids will be kids, but I think those kids are just cruel. It's the first day of school, and I have nothing new. Dad's trying hard, and Mom fills us up with love. Can you help my Dad get a job real soon? There's not many meals you can make out of love. I'm getting dressed for school, I'll study hard till the end of June.

I'll say a little prayer for my family and me as soon as I sit down in home room. Some of us kids don't have a happy story to tell, and it's not our faults if we don't. Some kids feel sorry for themselves. I'm not going to do that, I won't. I hear my parents downstairs, they're screaming and shouting with joy. Sounds like Dad found a job in the newspaper. That news would make me a happy young boy, Mr. President. If this job doesn't work out, can you please find my Dad a good job? I promise I'll do my best to be a good citizen and kid, your supporter, and friend.

Love,
Bob

Queen of the Sideline

Shawny was an only child with a disability. No one ever picked her for any game.
When the girls little league played, she roamed the sidelines. she looked sad and lonely, sometimes she was in pain
She'd shuffle back and forth, looking down at her braces, sometrimes looking up with a smile.
One day, the girls' team had a baseball game. Walking the sideline was Shawny, her mind was away a thousand miles. The coach of the little league team gathered the girls and asked, "Will you let that little girl play?"
The girls looked at each other and then all thumbs went up. They were all in agreement that day.
In the last inning, the team would let her hit. They gave her a jersey and a cap, And proudly on the bench she wouild sit. In the last inning with one out to go, the game was tied one to one., Shawny walked crookedly up to the plate.

She never dreamed she'd ever have this much fun. The pitcher pitched the ball while Shawny adjusted her hat.
"Strike one!" the umpire yelled as shawny lifted her bat.
The second pitch came, and Shawny made contact. you should have seen her face.
then the catcher picked up the ball and threw it too far, it went twenty feet past first base.
Onto second base, Shawny struggled, as the outfielder fumbled with the ball.
Half way to third, Shawny picked herself up, after she stumbled and refused to crawl.
On the way to home plate with the crowd screaming with cheers, the other teams catcher's eyes filled with tears, helped Shawny score on that beautiful play. The team made Shawny a captain, and Shawny made both teams proud winners that day.

Dear Mom and Dad,

By the time you read this letter, I'll be far away from here. I'm writing this to tell you how I feel. If you come to miss me, so what! I don't really care. I'm leaving, and this time it's for real. I don't want to go to school every single day, and being in bed by ten is for the birds.

I have slept enough, and what I have to say about school there simply are no words. I made it to the fifth grade, I deserve a rest. I tried to see it your way. I tried. I tried my best. I'm going to miss you two, but I just have to go.

Don't try to figure out where I'm going, I don't even know. I know what your thinking, but I won't be over Sue's. I called Sue this morning, she's leaving with me too. She says she's tired of cleaning and making up her bed, and if she washes one more dish, she's going to wind up dead. Oh, boy . . . I just thought of something.

We won't have any dishes 'cause we won't have a home, or we won't be able to call you guys 'cause we won't have a phone. Dad, can't take me fishing, he won't know where I'm at. And we won't be able to try out my new baseball and my bat. Even though Sue's really cute, Mom, she can't take the place of you, and plus you guys really need me.

I think I better call Sue.

Simply the Best

I wish I was a football star, my number would be 9
I'd run and jump and throw real far, I'd win all the time
Or I could be a baseball star, I'd hit that ball real hard
I'd be rich and buy my mom a bright red shiny car
Or I could be a basketball star, I'd shoot and never miss
All those girls would chase me down and try to get a kiss
Guess it wasn't meant to be, 'cause I can't run fast or throw a ball
I can't even hit a home run over that outfield wall
'Cause I'm in a wheelchair, I have a disability
But my mom and dad cheer me on, that means a lot to me
My dad pushes me in my wheelchair to each and every game
I carefully watch the players, I know their numbers and their names
I can't pick a favorite player, I have two or three
Guess who my dad's hero is, you guessed it, that's right, it's me

The Pots Melting

I'm part African American, Italian, and Jew
It's hard for me to be prejudice at all
Blacks can hate Whites, Whites can hate Jews
Short people can even hate the tall
There's been hated groups since the beginning of time
I've finally found a group who deserves the back of the line
I'll hate people who hate other people
This way I can be a hateful guy
I haven't had much practice at hating
It's going to be hard, but I'll give it a try
I'll try to get others to think like I do
I'll get them to hate people who hate people too
I love that idea, yes that's what I'll do
I hope you're not hateful, I'd hate to have to hate you!

Backward March

Sergeant Strongarm, I don't want to go to war with you
I didn't join the Army for that kind of thing
I'm not a trained killer, I'm peaceful, unlike you
Their scrawny necks, you talk about, I don't want to wring
This whole war thing, I just don't get it
I'm friendly I don't want to get out there and fight
Tell the fellas on the front line I said "What's up"
Sarge on you're way out, be a pal and turn out the lights
Bye now, don't let me hold you up . . .
I'm going to stay here, and catch up on my rest
Come on Sarge, don't look at me like that.
and please remove your hands from my neck
You'll have to wait if you want me to find my gun
I'll carry it, but don't expect me to use it
Alright alright, I'm coming, you guys aren't any fun . . . .

Fred

We just ate Fred, our family pet pig
I must admit Fred was a treat
As pigs go he was pretty big
He was a buddy of mine, but to Dad, he was just meat
Dad said one of us would have to slaughter him
So I flipped a coin with my brother Lou
I chose heads but it came up tails
I chased poor Fred with an axe for an hour or two
I chased him but, he was fast, that old Fred
I found out how fast when he started chasing me
That pig chased me till he fell over dead
A few more minutes, that chase would have killed me
We have another pet pig, he`s a fine stout thing
He's a nervous wreck that poor guy
He shakes every time we go near his pig pen
He doesn't seem to trust us, I can't imagine why?

Lucky Me

When the little hand's on the three and the big
    one's on the four
The school bell's going to ring, and I am
    running out this classroom door
It's the end of June, and it's school vacation,
    that's right yes, siree
There ain't gonna be no more rules or teachers
    to bother me
I don't need no education, I'm smart to be my age
I tricked those stupid teachers, and these silly books
    I didn't read one page
I have two months to lay around, that's right, I'll
    play and sleep
Soon as that stupid bell rings, I'm leaving
    without a peep
Why did they invent this goofy school stuff anyway
There's better things I can do, than be in school
    all day

Look at these kids around me, they think they
    can learn better than me
I don't need this school stuff to get rich, just
    wait, you'll see
I got kicked out of school seventeen times, so
    what, who needs this place
They laugh at me for not having nice clothes,
    that's why I punch them in the face
I'm always late for school 'cause Mom drinks
    and Dad does the same thing too
I wish I could be like those other kids, I wish that
    I was loved too
I don't get hugged or told that I'm loved, and
    that makes me really sad
When I grow up I'm gonna be the best parent any
    kid has ever had
Any of you, kids, who have a family that loves
    you, be nice and respect them everyday
And remember to be thankful that your life's
    better than mine
The next time you have a bad day

6 Going on 60

Santa, where's your reindeer? Are they parked outside? Maybe if you have sometime, you can take me for a ride. Can you take me to your sleigh when you're through working at this store? I wrote and asked for ten gifts but could you bring me more? Well, here comes Mom to get me, thanks for letting me sit on your lap. We're getting ready to go home now; I have to take my nap. Now, Santa, when you come down my chimney with my nice new little pup, if I'm asleep when you get there, you better to wake me up. You come and eat our cookies. You drink our milk and tea. Without as much as a howdy do, you turn around and leave! My Dad`s no help; I asked him to keep you in the house.

And Mom just watches you come down the chimney, then go up and go right out. Why are you so sneaky? What do you have to have hide? Last year you promised you'd wake me up, I'm beginning to think you lied. What's all the tip toeing about? What don't you want me to see? I already know you steal candy canes off our Christmas tree. You wait right here, I'm going to ask my mom if I can stay until you're through. I'm not taking any chances; I'm keeping an eye on you. There's nothing you can say to make me change my mind. I don't care if you're upset that I'm holding up the line. You say if I don't go, you'll put me on the list of kids that are bad. Santa, I love you. And I'm leaving right now. Please forget every thing I said.

Angels without Wings

Mom says we're all angels born without wings, It makes it easier for women to give birth.
She says we keep most of our heavenly things, But we lose the wings on our way down to earth.
As we grow up, it's our minds that learn to fly, She says we're perfectly pure from the start.
But she says when we tell our parents lies, It burdens our once pure hearts.
She says if we're good, our spirits rise.
And what we do with our life is up to us.
She says I'm her angel, but I just can't fly.
I wish I could, I really hate that school bus.
She told me to be an angel to my friends and family Be respectful, considerate and polite I believe every thing she says about angels, because I've never seen Anything with two wings in a fight

That's Disgusting

I pick noses for a living, it's a dirty job but it has to be done.
I've had better jobs in the past, but this one's a lot of fun.
There's big noses, small noses, fat and thin.
I love my job so much, there`s times I really dig in.
It takes a special kind of guy to pick a nose the way that I can.
It takes the same amount of time to pick a woman's nose as it does to pick a mans.
I have an assistant who helps me,
We both are nose picking pros.
When people hear what I do for a living,
they usually turn up their nose.
But they seem really relieved when I admit I pick noses with my eyes, for TV.
I choose the right noses for tissue commercials, I work for an advertising agency.
You may think, the way I trick people, by saying I pick noses is an utter disgrace, but it was so funny when I said, "I pick noses" to see that expression you had on your face.

The Gambler: 2nd grade can be tough

I bet this boy at school,
That you would bring me a bike.
Santa, I thought we were cool,
I lost and can't pay, so he wants to fight.
He said you wouldn't come through,
I bet him a dime that you would.
Santa, I'm frantic because of you, My heart's beating twice as
    fast as it should.
He said you didn't exist,
He said that you weren't for real.
Santa, I don't possess the skills, That's needed to survive this ordeal.
He said there's a way to get out of this debt, And a good
    chance I can double my money.
I've got inside information so I'm taking this bet, And putting
    a whole quarter on the Easter Bunny

AUTHOR BIO

Larry has a unique style. His poetry is written in story form. He has a lot to say and, he likes to express his observations of life and people in a light, easy flowing way. Larry was born in Pittsburgh, Pennsylvania. He is retired from the city of Pittsburgh Public Works Department where he worked with his brothers Ed and Paul. He had thirty three years of service and now that he has time, writes short stories and poetry. Larry and Paul attended Cheyney State College. His brother Ed an astute business man, attended Carnegie Mellon University is retired and living in Florida. His brother Paul teaches at a local college. Larry is the third child of Mary Louise And his late father Edward`s nine children. Larry has four brothers and four sisters.

As you read his poems, you'll find Larry's humor and sincerity refreshing. The poems are funny, thought-provoking and inspirational. These poems are for everyone. Larry will take you on a fun-filled ride you'll enjoy Larry's next book will explore more of our world and our fellow mans thoughts and actions, leaving a smile on your face and tugging a little at your heartstrings.

Made in the USA
Columbia, SC
30 January 2022